BEFORE I COULD UNDERSTAND

SUSAN ZELT

Copyright © 2025 by Susan Zelt.
All rights reserved.
No portion of this book may be reproduced in any form without written permission from the publisher or author, except as permitted by U.S. copyright law.

She was there, the day I was born...

...before I could understand.

She held me tight and kissed my head...

She knew God had a plan for me...

...before I could understand.

She cared for me when I was sick and sad...

She played blocks and puzzles and cars with me...

...before I could understand.

She tied my shoes and zipped my jacket...

...before I could understand.

She took me on walks and played at the park...

...before I could understand.

She read me books and tickled me...

...before I could understand.

She came to my games, recitals and plays...

...before I could understand.

She made my favorite things to eat...

...before I could understand.

She always smiled and hugged me close...

...before I could understand.

She told me Jesus loves me...

...before I could understand.

She taught me to pray and to be thankful...

She showed me how to love
with my heart...

...now I understand.

www.ingramcontent.com/pod-product-compliance
Lightning Source LLC
Chambersburg PA
CBHW041404010526
44107CB00015B/1065